A MAXTON BOOK ABOUT

FLOWERS

in woods and fields

by
Irma Wilde

Maxton Publishing Corporation
New York

Spring Beauty

When spring comes to the fields and woodlands, that is the time to look for the first wild flowers. Watch for sunny places in the woods, and there in the moist ground you will see hundreds of little pinkish-white flowers.

They are veined with a slightly darker pink, and bloom on frail, very crooked stems often close to the ground.

Although very delicate, it is the first flower to bloom.

At night this plant closes its starry flowers and goes to sleep! The flowers also close up when they are picked and never open again. Remember this when you pick them.

LIBRARY OF CONGRESS CATALOG CARD NUMBER: 52-3959   12345678962

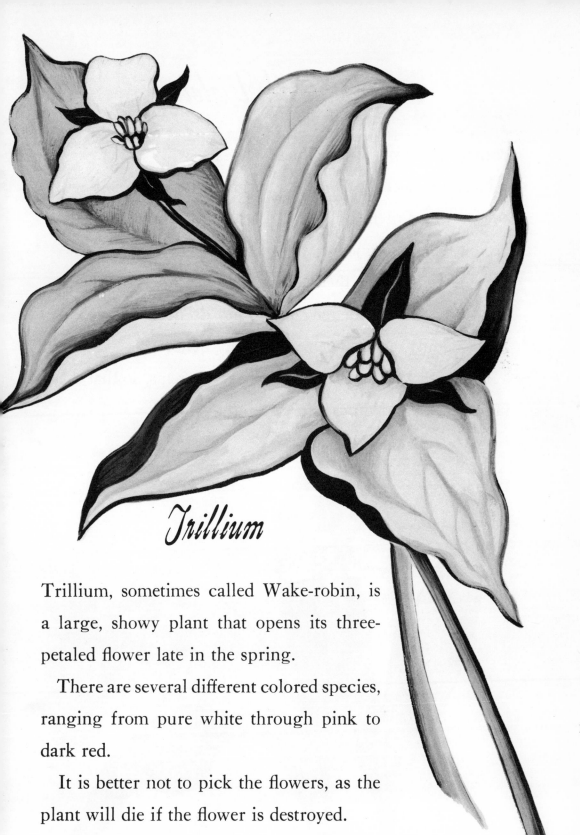

Trillium

Trillium, sometimes called Wake-robin, is a large, showy plant that opens its three-petaled flower late in the spring.

There are several different colored species, ranging from pure white through pink to dark red.

It is better not to pick the flowers, as the plant will die if the flower is destroyed.

Later the flowers are replaced by red or purple berries.

Dogtooth Violet

Perhaps there is a stream in your woods.

Near the water, where the ground becomes moist and boggy, you will find Dogtooth Violets blooming in large groups. Can you smell their sweet perfume?

Some people call them Adderstongues or Trout Lilies, which is perhaps a better name. They do not belong to the Violet family, as has been universally believed.

Dogtooth Violets always turn on their stems, so that they face the sun, and almost close at night.

Bluebells

Bluebells are beautiful blue bell-shaped flowers that grow in clumps by a stream or in moist, rich soil. The buds are pink and turn blue only after the flowers open.

This plant can easily be moved into your garden and will bloom there in all its beauty if it is done carefully.

Always wrap the roots so that the air will not dry them.

Wild Morning Glory

Get up early some summer morning and you will see the pink and white trumpets of the Morning Glories blooming in fields and meadows and twining about low bushes and fence posts. They grow in every kind of soil.

After a while, when the dew has disappeared and the sun is very hot, the flowers close.

Each flower blooms for just one day. Next morning a new lot will open and add their color to the scene.

Bloodroot

Be careful you do not step on these flowers. They are so easily bruised that even the wind will spoil them sometimes.

They like to grow in shaded, protected places in the woods, in rich soil.

The stems and roots of bloodroot contain an orange-red sap. The Indians used this sap to dye their blankets.

They also used it to make war paint.

Wild Columbine

Columbine flowers are like little ballet skirts of gold and scarlet.

You will find them growing in rocky wooded places.

The name Columbine comes from the Latin word *"columba,"* which means "dove." The petals resemble doves.

Violets

Wherever the sun can strike through the woods, even if for just a little while each day, you will see the blue and purple of Violets.

There are many different kinds of Violets. Some are light blue, others a dark purple. And if you look very hard you may find white and yellow Violets.

Some varieties are faintly scented, especially the white ones. The leaves of different species vary too.

Lupine

The Lupine has leaves like many-fingered hands.

The pea-like flowers, usually blue, are really five petals joined together and grow on a tall stem.

Lupines are usually found in grassy meadows. They are often cultivated in gardens and, with very little care, will grow there just as well as in the meadows.

Red Clover

This flower is the favorite of the honey bees, for the flower heads are made up of many tiny tubular florets each filled with a treat for the bees.

There are several different kinds of clover but nearly all have the familiar three-leaflet leaves.

At night the Red Clover leaflets fold down to sleep.

Trailing Arbutus

Look closely under the spruce and pine trees. There, almost buried in last year's leaves, you will find the pale pink flowers of the lovely, fragrant Trailing Arbutus. This is known as the Mayflower of the Pilgrims.

Nearby nodding blue violets are growing among the mosses and waiting to be picked. These, with the lovely Arbutus may be made into tiny fragrant bouquets. Both of these flowers will keep in water for some time. But be very careful how you pick the Trailing Arbutus. If the plant is pulled up by the roots there will not be any to bloom next spring. This flower is becoming increasingly scarce in many places because people have carelessly torn its roots up, thereby destroying it.

Wild Aster

Autumn has come.

Wild Asters are blooming in the fields and along the edges of the woods. They look like purple and blue smoke among the fallen leaves.

There are many different kinds, and the color varies from white, blue to purple.

The plants are tall and carry their flowers high.

Great Mullein

Here is another tall plant, taller than the wild Asters. It holds its light yellow flowers, like a candle, high on a stout stem. There is a cluster of large soft leaves at the roots.

Only a few flowers open at a time.

Adam's Flannel is another name for the Great Mullein.

Wild Strawberry

Hugging the ground, and sometimes growing beneath other plants, you will find wild strawberries. But remember where they grow, for when the berries are ripe they are sweet and children love to pick them and eat them.

The birds love them, too!

Butter and Eggs

Everyone knows these flowers, like tiny Snap-dragons. Only the bumblebees can gather the honey. The large orange "lip" closes the flower but the bumblebee is heavy enough to make the "lip" open when it lights upon the flower.

Squeeze one of the flowers gently and it will open its mouth and snap it shut when you let go.

Jack-in-the-Pulpit

Every child knows "Jack," standing tall among the ferns and flowers.

It likes best the moist ground near a stream and blooms with the Spring Beauties.

The root and the bright red berries of Jack-in-the-Pulpit are edible when boiled. They were eaten by the Indians.

Buttercup

You think of butter when you see a Buttercup.

Children hold Buttercups beneath each other's chins to see the yellow light reflected from the shiny golden petals.

Some Buttercups bloom only in the spring, but other species flower all summer long in meadows and moist ground.

A long time ago in England, which was the home of our Buttercup, it was spelled "Buttercop." "Cop" meant button. The French name today means "golden buttons."

Jewelweed

Do you like to wade along a shallow stream? On the banks and nodding over the water are the lovely flowers of the Jewelweed.

This plant is a favorite of the hummingbirds and they will often be seen darting from flower to flower gathering the sweet nectar.

Some people call it Touch-me-not, because the ripe seedpods burst at the slightest touch.

Forget-Me-Not

Look under the Jewelweed.

There you will find the sky-blue sprays of Forget-me-nots.

They like the wet, cool soil by a stream in partially shaded spots and will even root their stems in the water.

Milkweed

Look for the brown and orange Monarch Butterflies. You will find them hovering about the Milkweed blossoms.

The flowers are lilac colored, and if you have picked any of them you will find your fingers are sticky with the white milky sap that gives this plant its name.

In the fall the pods of white silk will burst and carry their seeds afar on little puffs of down.

Queen Anne's Lace

Summer is well along now.

Bees and insects hum and the sun is hot. Weeds and grasses are tall, and waving above them all is the frothy Queen Anne's Lace. It is also called Wild Carrot.

There is a single purple floret in the center of each flower cluster. The flower, when opened, has a lace-like form.

It is sometimes called Bird's Nest, for, as the flowers age, they curl up in the shape of a green "bird's nest."

Yellow Pond Lily

The wild yellow Pond Lily has been blooming all summer and now there are great masses of leaves and flowers in the quiet, shallow pools. Water Lilies do not like the fast-flowing water of the stream.

The flower is fragrant, hardy, and lovely. Long ago the seeds were sometimes used as food by the Indians.

Another name for the Yellow Pond Lily is Spatter Dock.

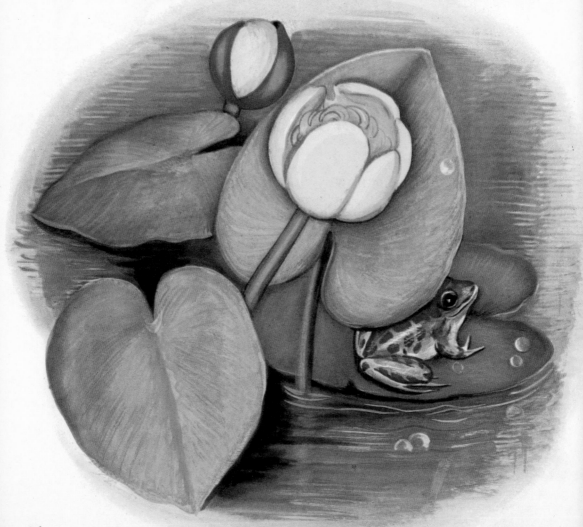

*Bottle
Gentian*

Growing near the stream you will find the blue flowers of the Bottle or Closed Gentian.

Bees and other insects have a hard time forcing their way into these flowers.

Other members of the Gentian family have differently shaped flowers, such as the vase-like fringed flowers of the Fringed Gentian. The colors are blue to violet.

A medicine is made from the roots of the Gentian.

The flowers are rare and should not be picked. Neither will the plant thrive if transplanted to a garden.

Bittersweet

The last autumn leaf is covered with snow and the flowers have long since disappeared.

As you fly over the field and past the woods on your sled, it is hard to believe that flowers were all blooming here such a short time ago.

Yet there on the fencepost is a Bittersweet Vine. Its orange and yellow berries are eagerly sought by the birds for food.

It has been named Bittersweet because its taste at first is bitter and then sweet.

Partridgeberry

And in the woods, not far from a protecting thicket, shine some bright red Partridgeberries, or Twinberries.

Next spring this evergreen vine will be covered with pale pinkish-white flowers which bloom in pairs, or "twins."

The flowers are all there waiting for the cold winds and snows to go. Soon spring will come again and wake them to bloom once more.

Wild Roses and Bluets

Do you enjoy running through the fields in the warm mid-summer days? Perhaps something scratched your legs. If so, you may find wild Roses for they have thorns just like the garden Roses.

One of the wild Roses, the Sweetbriar, was brought to this country by the Pilgrims.

The flowers of all the wild Roses have a sweet perfume and even the leaves of the Sweetbriar are fragrant.

Look under the tall plants. There, if you hunt carefully, you may find some dainty little blue flowers called Bluets. Some people call them Quaker Ladies.

Can you guess why?